Just Write

Creativity and Craft in Writing

Book 3

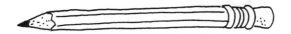

Elsie S. Wilmerding • Alexandra S. Bigelow

illustrations by George Ulrich

EDUCATORS PUBLISHING SERVICE
Cambridge and Toronto

Acknowledgments
Thank you to our husbands, Ned Bigelow and Patrick Wilmerding,
who have been so supportive.
Also, a special thanks to fifth-grade teacher Sarah Shields.

Acquisitions/Development: Sethany Rancier

Editor: Elissa Gershowitz

Typesetting: Persis B. Levy

Managing Editor: Sheila Neylon

ISBN 0-8388-2629-6

978-0-8388-2629-4

4 5 6 7 MLY 10 09 08 07

Contents

Introduction

Writing is a way to communicate and learn. When you write, your mind has to sort through many ideas and impressions to choose the words and writing style that will best convey your message. There are many different types of writing, just as there are many reasons to write.

Throughout this book, four main writing styles will be discussed: *narrative writing, descriptive writing, expository writing,* and *persuasive writing.* Reading and writing go hand in hand, and you will read models that show how others have expressed themselves. These examples will provide guidelines for your writing.

Kinds of Writing

There are four main kinds of writing: narrative, descriptive, expository, and persuasive.

- *Narrative writing* includes fictional and nonfiction stories, and personal histories. Examples are fairy tales, biographies, and newspaper stories.

- *Descriptive writing* focuses on describing a person, place, or thing, using the five senses. Poems can be examples of descriptive writing.

- *Expository writing* is meant to show something new to your audience. Information reports and paragraph summaries are examples of expository writing. Lists and directions are also expository writing.

- *Persuasive writing* means trying to convince someone of something as a result of your writing. Letters to the editor and advertisements are two types of persuasive writing.

Reasons for Writing

One purpose of writing can be *narrative,* which means your writing tells the story of something or someone real or imaginary.

Another reason to write is to *describe* something for someone else—your reader. Much of what we write is descriptive. Descriptive writing paints a mental picture for the reader.

The purpose of writing can also be *expository,* giving information about a topic like a period in history, a scientific discovery, or a significant individual. In school, you are often asked to write *summaries* in your own words, to help you absorb and learn what you have read.

Sometimes your writing needs to be *persuasive*. This means trying to convince your readers to have the same opinion as you.

Some writing is used for the purpose of entertainment. Can you think of some stories and books you have read for fun?

In *Just Write 3*, you will be introduced to the four styles of writing. Each will be useful to you at different times and for different reasons. The rules often overlap, but the tone of each one—narrative, descriptive, expository, and persuasive—should be distinct.

On page 88 at the end of the book is a Story Bank where you can keep story ideas to use in your writing. When doing the writing exercises, if you need more room to write, attach another paper to the page.

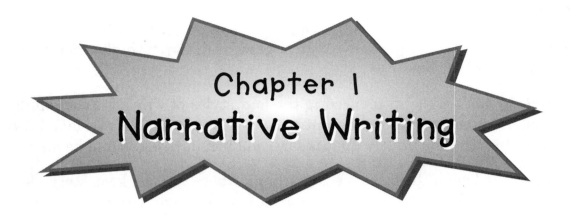
Chapter 1
Narrative Writing

Let's begin with *narrative* writing. A narrative tells a story made up of events that flow together to form a beginning, middle, and end. It is usually composed of many paragraphs. Common types of narratives are *fictional* (made-up) stories, *personal narratives*, and *nonfiction* stories.

Reviewing Story Elements

In *Just Write 1* and *Just Write 2*, you practiced working with the three basic elements of a narrative story.

- **character:** The character or characters do the action in the story. The characters don't have to be people; they can be animals or objects.

- **setting:** The setting tells where and when the story takes place.

- **plot:** The plot is the action of the story. It is often based on a central problem that has to be solved. The *plot line* is a like a map; it shows the main events of the story rising to a climax and then coming down to a resolution or conclusion.

Fictional Stories

Fictional stories are made up by the author. Authors use their imaginations to tell stories about interesting characters, settings, and plots.

Read the story on the next page.

A Rainy Day

It was a rainy Sunday in September. Ten-year-old Lina and her little cousin Max were stuck inside. They watched sadly as raindrops dripped down the outside of the windowpanes. Lina and Max were supposed to go to the country fair, but the rain kept them home and indoors.

"I'm bored," whined Max after five minutes. He was seven years old and loved to ride his bike and play outside. "There's nothing to do!"

Lina sighed. They were spending the whole afternoon together, and she knew what Max could be like when he was grumpy. "Let's ask my parents for ideas," Lina suggested.

Lina's parents were reading a newspaper in the living room. "We don't have anything to do," Lina and Max complained.

"Why don't you straighten up your room?" said Lina's mother, smiling.

"No…" they both said.

"Why don't you wash the breakfast dishes?" suggested Lina's father, laughing.

"No!" said Lina and Max.

"Then use your imaginations," Lina's mother said.

Lina and Max went back to the playroom. "I've got it!" said Lina. "Let's write a book!" She sat down at her desk and pulled out some paper, a pen, and colored pencils. "Let's think of a good story. I'll write, and you can draw the pictures," she said.

Max sat down beside her. "Can we write a story about the country fair?" he sniffed.

"Yes, let's write about what we would have seen if we'd been able to go."

"Can I pretend we ran into space aliens there?" asked Max.

"Sure," said Lina, giggling. "Mom told us to use our imaginations!"

Lina and Max passed the afternoon working on their story. After writing the last sentence, Lina read the story out loud. Together, they revised the parts they didn't like or that didn't make sense. Then, they bound the book using some yarn and glue, and took it to the living room to show Lina's parents.

When Max's family came to pick him up later that afternoon, his smile was as bright as the sun that had just come out. "We wrote a book," he said proudly, "and Lina's going to help me write another one the next time there's a rainy day!"

Reading Response

Can you identify the main elements of the story? Fill in the boxes below. You do not need to write in complete sentences.

Characters

_____

Setting

_____

Plot

problem? _____

_____

events? _____

_____

Dialogue

Dialogue is the talking that takes place between the characters in a story. Having dialogue in your story helps bring your characters to life. Dialogue is also a way to get your story moving from one event to the next.

Changing Paragraphs for a New Speaker

When people are having a conversation or dialogue, a new speaker begins a new paragraph. This helps readers keep track of who is speaking and what each person is saying. Turn back to *A Rainy Day*. Notice that the paragraphs change each time a different person speaks.

 For review exercises and practice with changing paragraphs for a new speaker and punctuating dialogue, turn to page 78.

Remember When punctuating dialogue:

- Put quotation marks before the first word spoken and after the last word spoken.

- Use commas to separate spoken words from the speaker.

- Capitalize the first word after the quotation mark at the beginning of a sentence.

- If the quotation is interrupted midsentence, the first letter of the second clause is lowercase.

- Punctuation marks go <u>inside</u> the quotation marks.

Remember Don't forget to indent every new paragraph.

Exercise Using Dialogue

Write a brief five-line dialogue between two people. For example, you might invent a scene where two people are discussing homework or making plans for the weekend. Or, feel free to create your own imaginative scene.

_____

_____

_____

_____

_____

_____

✔ Editing Checklist ✔

❑ Did you start a new paragraph every time the speaker changed?

❑ Is all of your punctuation within the quotation marks?

❑ Did you remember to capitalize the first words of the sentences and use lowercase if a sentence is continuing?

Chronology

In many stories the most logical way to present events is in *chronological order*. This means that each event is shown in the order it happened. Often, there are signal words or phrases that indicate a shift in time or in an event.

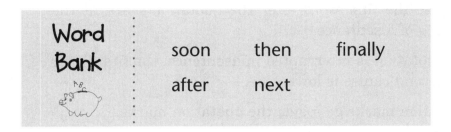

Word Bank

soon   then   finally

after   next

Exercise : Chronological Order

The first thing that happens in the story *A Rainy Day* is: <u>Max and Lina watch the</u> <u>rain falling outside.</u>

The next thing that happens is: <u>Max complains that there is nothing to do.</u>

The third event is: <u>Max and Lina ask Lina's parents for help.</u>

Then, the cousins decide to spend their afternoon: _____

_____

Finally,: _____

_____

Changes in Time

Notice that the story is broken into paragraphs. A new paragraph may indicate a change in time: different events happening as time passes. Read the story again, and notice the time shifts.

✎ Practice

Go back and underline the signal words that indicate changes in time in the story *A Rainy Day* on page 3.

Exercise Changes in Time

What is the difference in time between the first and second paragraphs? What words tell you that a change in time has occurred?

_____

What is the difference in time between the last paragraph and the one right before it? What words tell you that a change has occurred?

_____

Changes in Topic

A new paragraph can also indicate a change in topic. When the subject shifts from one thing to another, it is usually time to start a different paragraph.

Exercise Changes in Topic

The story below is written as one paragraph, but it actually should be two. Insert a paragraph mark (¶) where you think the topic changes and the second paragraph should begin.

Dreaming of Pirates

Josh awoke with a start. He had been dreaming of pirates again! For the past week, Josh's dreams all involved pirates. In one dream, a huge pirate ship sailed up the street to his school, taking him on an adventure involving gold and treasure. Another dream included a mean pirate who made Josh swab the deck of the ship. He couldn't understand why he was having so many dreams about pirates. Then, Josh remembered that his class had read a poem about pirates at the beginning of the week. He had been fascinated by the lives of these outlaws of the sea. He decided to start keeping a dream diary so he would remember his imaginary pirate adventures. One day maybe he'd turn his stories into a book!

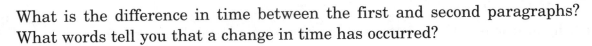

Exercise : New Paragraphs

1. Carefully read the paragraph below and indicate with the paragraph sign (¶) where each new paragraph should begin. Think about chronology, changes in time and topic, dialogue, and different speakers.

2. Next, add the missing punctuation (commas, quotations marks, questions marks, periods) within the dialogue. Then, think about a conclusion for the story.

A Camping Trip

William thinks camping with his grandparents is great fun. They always bring a map, compass, flashlight, first-aid kit, and bug repellent, as well as a tent, sleeping bags, and food. They also toast marshmallows at night, and tell stories around the fire. One day last May, the weather was perfect. William's grandfather strapped his canoe to the top of the car—or so he thought. As they were driving along, William heard a bumping sound in the back. Hey, what's that noise? I have no idea said Grandpa we'd better take a look. They pulled over to the side of the road to check. The canoe had slipped backwards and was flopped over to the side.

Explain why there is a need for changes in paragraphs throughout the story.

_____

Did the story seem to end abruptly, without warning? Go back and write a conclusion to this story. You may need to start a new paragraph.

_____

_____

_____

_____

_____

Titles

It is important for every narrative story to have a *title*. A title tells the readers what the story is about. The title should be short—only a few words—and informative but interesting. Since it is the first thing readers see, the title should make them curious enough to want to read the whole story.

Remember Capitalize every word in the title, expect for articles in the middle of the title (*a, an, the*) and prepositions (also known as "linking words," such as *with, of, between*).

Exercise : Writing a Fictional Story

Now it's your turn to write a fictional story. Use the Brainstorming Box below to plan and develop your ideas. As you brainstorm, think about the basic elements of a story: characters, setting, and plot. Also keep in mind dialogue and chronological order. Next, fill in the story map on the next page. Finally, you are ready to write your story!

Brainstorming Box

Story Map

Topic: _____

Characters:

Setting:

Problem:

Action 1:

Action 2:

Conclusion:

Title: _____

_____

_____

_____

_____

_____

_____

_____

_____

_____

_____

_____

_____

_____

_____

_____

_____

_____

✓ Editing Checklist ✓

- ❑ Did you put the events of your story in logical order?

- ❑ Did you use dialogue?

- ❑ Do you have new paragraphs where necessary?

Personal Narratives

Another type of narrative writing is a *personal narrative*. Personal narratives follow the same basic rules as fictional stories, but instead of being made-up they tell a true story about the author. A personal narrative is written from the *first-person* point of view. That means the author is the *narrator*.

Who is the narrator?

- **First-person:** The story is about the person who is writing it. An autobiography is usually written in first-person. First-person narration often uses the words "I," "me," "my," "our," "us," or "we" to tell who is doing the action.

- **Third-person:** The story is told by someone else about the main character. Key words to identify third-person narration include "he," "him," "she," "her," "they," "them," and "their" when describing who is doing the action.

As you read the following story, think about what makes it a personal narrative.

Going Onstage

When I think back to that old house my family lived in until I was six years old, it makes me laugh to remember the hilarious times my sister and I had. We especially loved playing dress-up in the attic. There was a big trunk of funny, old-fashioned clothes that my parents and grandparents had saved.

One time, we put on shiny purple satin dresses with white beads, hats with blue feathers, and high-heeled shoes. We also had lots of fun with our mom's makeup. We ended up looking like two peacocks! Our neighbor came over and took pictures. They later appeared on the school bulletin board, and everyone laughed at us. At first we felt so embarrassed, but then we laughed, too.

We also wrote plays that were so silly we couldn't keep a straight face when acting. There were old curtains hanging up in the attic, so we made a stage and even charged a quarter for admission! One time, our audience was Mom and our dog. Mom couldn't stop laughing throughout the performance. "You should take the show on the road," she said.

"Maybe we will!" I replied. So off we went, across the street to Grandpa's house, dressed in our flowing clothes. It was hard to cross the street in our big shoes and clothes. I held my sister's hand tightly.

Grandpa wanted to see the play twice, he liked it so much. Ever since that time, my grandparents take us to a play once a year. For my last birthday, I saw *Peter Pan*. It was wonderful!

Reading Response

1. Who is narrating this story? Is it written in first-person or third-person?

   _____

2. Name two or three things you learned about the narrator from reading this story.

   _____

3. Think about the chronological order of events. Put a number 1 next to the first thing that happens, a 2 by the next, and so on.

   _____ a. The kids give a play in the attic.

   _____ b. The kids go to *Peter Pan*.

   _____ c. They walk across the street to Grandpa's house.

   _____ d. The kids dress up in long purple dresses.

Word Choice: Verbs

Choosing vivid verbs is important. Remember that verbs are like the engine of a sentence: a strong engine can pull a long train, but a weak one struggles. Also, don't use the same verb over and over. You want to find the verb that best describes the action.

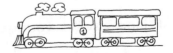

Remember Verbs are "action words" or "being words."

✏ Practice

Read this short example and underline the verbs.

The cowboy leaped on his horse, waved good-bye, and galloped down the road, kicking up stones and dust as he disappeared.

Add to the verb bank below by looking back at the previous stories in this book and picking some verbs you like. Then, add some of your own verbs. Write them in the bank below.

Word Bank	plodded	_____	_____
	staggered	_____	_____
	fretted	_____	_____

Exercise — Working with Verbs

Read each sentence below, and circle the verb you think best expresses the action.

1. Fernando *looked* down to the bottom of the deep, cavernous valley.

   admired   peered   glanced

2. As soon as the detective heard the frightening thump, she *climbed* upstairs to investigate.

   descended   flew   staggered

3. Feeling shy, he *went* behind his dad.

   fell   yawned   hid

4. Jane saw her younger brother *watching* from behind the tree.

   sneaking   spying   standing

Reading Response

Have you noticed that certain verbs can evoke certain feelings? Showing feelings in your writing makes your story come alive.

Read these two sentences:

> The panther charged through the forest.

> The panther snuck through the forest.

How do the verbs make the sentences differ in feeling?

_____

_____

Exercise | Writing a Personal Narrative

Write a personal narrative about a time when you were happy, trying something new, or when you felt sad or lonely. Show your feelings by choosing strong verbs (you can use your verb Word Bank on page 14 for ideas) and using details. Use the Brainstorming Box below to think of ideas, then fill in the Story Map on the next page before starting your personal narrative.

Brainstorming Box

Story Map

Topic: _____

Characters:	**Setting:**

Problem:

Action 1:

Action 2:

Conclusion:

Remember > Think about:

1. Who is telling the story.

2. The sequence of events.

3. Using interesting verbs.

Title: _____

_____

_____

_____

_____

_____

_____

_____

_____

_____

_____

_____

_____

_____

_____

_____

_____

_____

_____

_____

✓ **Editing Checklist** ✓

❑ Have you clearly shown who is the narrator?

❑ What are some of the interesting verbs you used? _____

_____

❑ What are some feelings you have conveyed? _____

_____

_____

Nonfiction Narratives

A *nonfiction narrative* is a type of story involving things that really happened. These can be historical events, such as scientific discoveries, or current events, such as news stories. Nonfiction narratives also include biographies: books written about real people from the past or present.

Newspaper Writing

A news report is one type of nonfiction narrative. It is generally told from the third-person perspective. This means that the story is relayed by someone who did not participate directly in the events.

 **Remember** First-person words: I, me, my, our, us, we

Third-person words: he, him, she, her, they, them

The *lead* is the opening of a news story. It's often the first line, and generally tells the main idea of the piece of news. The information the reporter gathers is structured around the Five Ws: *who what where when why.*

Read the following nonfiction narrative and think about the Five Ws.

Hurricane Dennis Hits the Southeast

Hurricane Dennis raced through the southeastern coast of Florida last night. It hit Jacksonville at approximately 8:00 p.m. and traveled up to Savannah, Georgia, before moving out to sea early this morning. Winds raced at ninety-five miles per hour, and the sea's swells reached as high as ten feet.

The damage from Hurricane Dennis was concentrated in the area just north of Jacksonville. Fortunately, most of the townspeople were evacuated, but coming home this afternoon, they found trees down, electrical power outages, and minor flooding. Schools were also closed.

The last time a hurricane of this magnitude hit was fifteen years ago. There was no warning, resulting in five deaths and as many as fifty people being hospitalized from injuries related to the hurricane. Luckily, weather technology has greatly improved. The warning for Dennis went out three days ago, so everyone knew of the impending storm.

There were no reports of any injuries, but some damage to property was indicated. Resident Stacey Richards reports that a tree fell on her car. "Unfortunately, it is damaged beyond repair," she said, "but most important, I am relieved and happy that my children and I are safe."

Reader Response

What is the *lead* of the story? _____

_____

Who was affected by the event? _____

(Continued on next page.)

What happened? _____

_____

Where did the event take place? _____

When did it happen? _____

Why was it known about ahead of time? _____

Exercise Nonfiction Narrative Writing

Pretend you are a reporter. First, think of an event that really happened, for example something from the news, a storm, a sporting event, or a school fundraiser. Fill in the chart below.

Use the Five Ws: *who, what, where, when, why* to help structure your newspaper article.

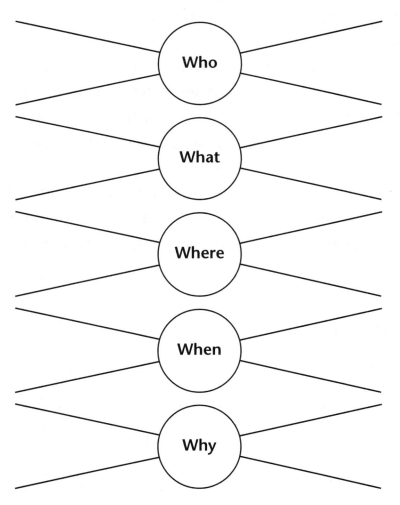

- Think of a good lead for your story.

- Use interesting verbs.

- Tell events in chronological order.

- Remember the Five Ws.

Now, write your nonfiction narrative news story.

Title: _____

_____

_____

_____

_____

_____

_____

_____

_____

_____

_____

_____

_____

✓ Editing Checklist ✓

❏ Does your lead grab the reader's attention and introduce the main point of your story?

❏ Did you describe the events in chronological order?

❏ Does your story answer the Five Ws?

Chapter 2
Descriptive Writing

Descriptive writing is frequently incorporated into many kinds of writing, such as fictional narratives, personal narratives, and nonfiction narratives. It can also be independent—its own category of writing.

The main goal of descriptive writing is to create a picture of a place, person, thing, or event in the mind of the reader. Words can set a tone or paint a picture by appealing to the *senses*. Descriptive words tell how things look, smell, sound, feel, and taste. Strong adjectives and adverbs help convey the message of the writing. Read the passage below. Notice how the narrator shows a specific image by choosing words that appeal to the senses.

School's Out!

Friday afternoon came at last. The world was bright and brimming with life. All the fields were fresh and green. Apple trees were in bloom, their fragrant blossoms filling the air. At the ringing of the school bell, the doors burst open. Loud, happy children emerged. School was out! Long, warm summer days lay ahead of them.

Reading Response

1. This passage is filled with sensory references. Circle the details or words that relate to the five senses.

2. Is this paragraph narrated in first-person or third-person?

_____

3. What is the setting of this paragraph? Draw a picture of it.

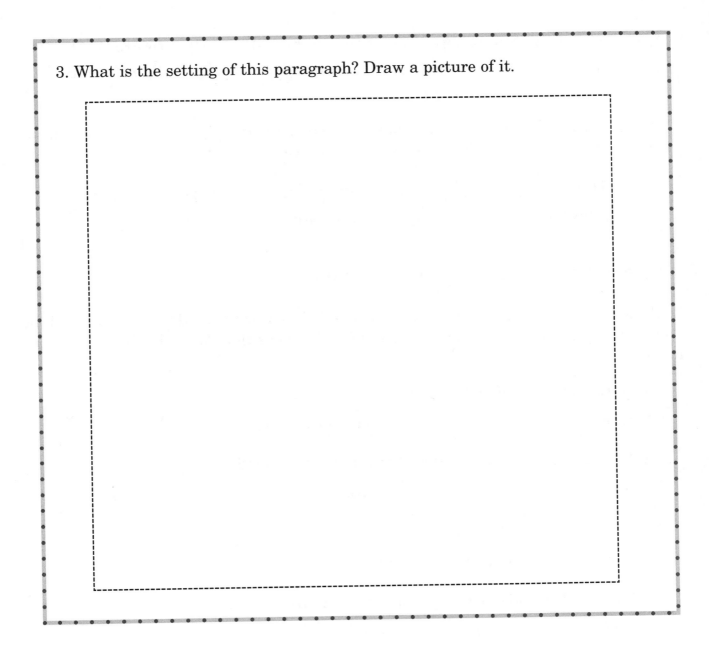

Details: Choosing Adjectives

Adding details and description is a good way to liven up your writing. The words you choose also reflect the mood or feeling of your story.

Do you remember what an *adjective* is? Adjectives are words that describe nouns. They can tell what color something is, its size, and how it looks, feels, sounds, smells, and tastes. Adjectives are a good way for writers to give details.

 When you choose adjectives, select your words carefully. Sometimes it's easy to get carried away with adjectives. Here is an example of adjective overload.

The silly, funny squirrel jammed his fat, puffy cheeks with delicious, brown nuts and scampered up the tall, red and orange, colorful tree.

In the sentence above, the writer has used too many adjectives. Cross out the unnecessary ones. Perhaps your sentence might end up reading like this:

The silly squirrel jammed his puffy cheeks with nuts and scampered up the tall, colorful tree.

Exercise Choosing Adjectives

In the following sentences, replace the *adjective* in italics with one that best describes the noun. Cross out the two that do not fit, and 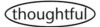 the one that does. The first one is done for you.

1. A *nice* neighbor offered to help.

   ~~selfish~~   ~~skillful~~   (thoughtful)

2. He could see that his younger sister was in a *bad* mood.

   happy   grumpy   nervous

3. The apple trees smelled *good*.

   sour   fragrant   bitter

4. The *cold* day made their fingers and toes numb.

   sweltering   timid   wintry

5. He noticed two *unclear* headlights.

   yellow   blurry   scary

Exercise Writing with Adjectives

Describe a place you know, choosing adjectives that use all your senses.

Place: _____

Sight	Smell	Sound	Touch	Taste

Now write about your place.

Title: _____

_____

_____

_____

_____

_____

_____

_____

✓ **Editing Checklist** ✓

❑ Did you use a variety of adjectives?

❑ Did you think about your senses?

❑ Did you describe the setting?

✎ Practice

Underline your sensory words. Do you need more? Did you use too many?

Word Choice: Adverbs

Adverbs, like adjectives, can help describe the actions and behaviors of characters, or help readers picture a setting. Just as adjectives describe nouns, adverbs help modify verbs, adjectives, or other adverbs. Adverbs often end in –ly, and they usually tell readers *when, where,* or *how*.

Read the description below. Notice how the writer conveys a specific image through descriptive adjectives and adverbs.

The Funny Clown

Everyone laughed yesterday when the clown, with his painted white face and funny, baggy pants, awkwardly entered the stage on six-foot stilts. He wobbled unsteadily to one side and then the other. His tall black hat fell off, but he never did.

Reading Response

What do you think the clown looks like? Read the paragraph again, and underline each word or phrase that describes the clown. Then, use the details to draw a picture of him.

Practice

What are two adjectives used in the description of the clown?

_____

What are two adverbs used in the description of the clown?

_____

Here is a word bank with adverbs. Add some of your own.

Word Bank	sadly	mysteriously	_____
	happily	_____	_____
	tomorrow	_____	_____

Exercise 1 Choosing Adverbs

Choose the best adverb for each sentence, and write it on the line. The verbs are in italics.

1. The girl *ran* _____ to the site of the accident.

   swiftly   mysteriously   humorously

2. They *played* _____ in the ocean.

   sorrowfully   joyfully   suddenly

3. The announcer *tripped* _____ as he opened the curtains.

   awkwardly   kindly   tomorrow

4. The little boy *moaned* _____ when his dad said it was time to go to bed.

   silently   miserably   cheerfully

Remember Adverbs usually answer the questions *When? Where?* or *How?*

Exercise 2 Choosing **When?** Adverbs

Here are some adverbs that answer the question *when.* Choose the one that best fits the sentence, and write it on the line.

1. _____ they will sail into the harbor.

   Yesterday   Tomorrow   Formerly

2. She _____ goes to school on Saturday.

   frequently   occasionally   never

Write two of your own sentences using *when* adverbs.

1. _____

2. _____

Exercise 3 : Choosing **Where?** Adverbs

Here are some adverbs that answer the question *where*. Choose the one that best fits the sentence, and write it on the line.

    1. The bird flew _____.

       outside   underneath   down

    2. The tower of cards fell _____.

       over   on   below

Write two of your own sentences using *where* adverbs.

1. _____

2. _____

Similes

Individual adverbs can answer the question *how*. Another way to answer *how* is to use a group of words called an *adverbial phrase*. Adverbial phrases describe people, places, or objects, often by making comparisons. For example, read the following sentence:

    She leapt from the chair like a frog.

The phrase "like a frog" is a *simile*, describing how the girl leapt from her chair. A *simile* is an indirect, unexpected comparison between two things. The words: "like" or "as" connect the two things.

Exercise ‹ Choosing Similes

Read the comparisons below, and circle the one that best ends the sentence. Then, write it on the line.

1. The boy jumped _____.

   like a snake

   like slippery silk

   as high as a skyscraper

2. The cookie dough felt _____.

   like squishy marshmallows

   like crispy tortilla shells

   like the moon

3. The heavy statue fell _____.

   like a chiming bell

   like a ton of bricks

   like a dozen glasses being dropped

Exercise ‹ Writing a Character Description

Think about someone you know. Imagine all the details you can about the person. Think of how he or she looks, sounds, dresses, and speaks. Use the web below to collect your details.

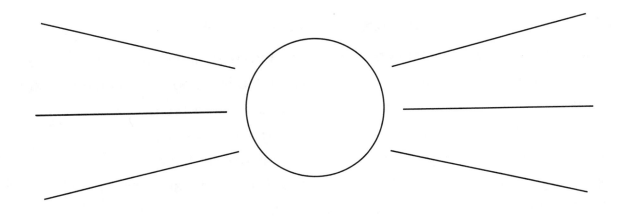

Now, write your descriptive paragraph.

Title: _____

_____

_____

_____

_____

_____

_____

✓ **Editing Checklist** ✓

❏ Did you use adverbs and adjectives?

❏ Did you use any similes?

Exercise Describing an Event

Read the two descriptions below. Watch for the words and phrases that help make the writing more interesting.

The Jazz Concert: Passage 1

We went to a concert last weekend. It was jazz music. We heard a great drummer, piano player, and clarinetist. We didn't get home until after 10:00 p.m. It was fun.

The Jazz Concert: Passage 2

Last Saturday night, my parents took me, my big sister, and some friends to a concert. Everyone in the group loved it! My mom sang loudly along with her old favorites. My sister and her friends were dancing in the aisle. Being a drummer, my dad tapped his fingers and toes along with the jazzy rhythms that zigged and zagged like birds. The piano player's fingers moved like lightning up and down the keyboard, but the clarinetist was my favorite. Her playing was as smooth as silk, sweeping the melody along like a wave. We got home late, but it was worth it!

1. Which passage is more interesting to read? Why?

_____

_____

Underline the details that added to the descriptions in each of the passages.

2. What senses does the narrator of the second passage use?

_____

3. To what does the narrator compare the piano player?

_____

Exercise Descriptions

Think of a place, person, or event to describe—perhaps, your bedroom, a friend, or a picnic. First create the details by filling out the chart below.

Sight	Smell	Sound	Touch	Taste

Think about how you will organize your writing. Now, write your description.

Title: _____

_____

_____

_____

_____

_____

_____

- ❑ Have you used interesting adjectives and adverbs?

- ❑ Did you choose sensory words?

- ❑ Do you want to change anything?
  Circle a description you think you could improve.

Poetry

Poetry is a special kind of descriptive writing. A poem can explore, express, or describe an emotion, experience, idea, or memory. Poems are usually short descriptions that are packed with rich, imaginative language. A poem reflects the essence of a feeling, experience, or idea through chosen words and phrases.

Below is a series of words from the descriptive paragraph about the jazz concert on page 30. This shows how you can pull out imaginative phrases and rich language to begin to build a poem.

Jazz Concert

Fingers moving
like lightning,
up and down.
Jazzy rhythms
zigged and zagged like birds,
smooth as silk,
sweeping the melody.

Notice how the feeling of the concert is conveyed in these few phrases and images.

Poetry comes in many forms. The words at the end of each line of poetry sometimes rhyme, but often they don't.

Similes and Metaphors

Comparing two things using *similes* or *metaphors* helps the writer create poetic images that draw pictures in readers' minds.

 **Remember** A *simile* compares two things using the words *like* or *as* to connect them:

> The player's fingers were moving along the piano *like* lightning.

> My feet are warm *as* toast.

A *metaphor* is related to a simile, but it compares two things directly, without using the connecting words *like* or *as*:

> Her heart is a stone.

> Our school is a maze.

Similes and metaphors help readers picture things in an unexpected way by comparing two things not typically thought of together. For example, by comparing "fingers" with "lightning," the "Jazz Concert" poet makes us think of the player's fingers as moving quickly and with great force, sharing some of the qualities of lightning.

✎ Practice

Here are some examples of similes and metaphors. <u>Underline</u> the two things being compared. Then decide if each example is a simile or a metaphor, and circle the correct answer.

The wind pressed the <u>grass</u> flat as a <u>pancake</u>.   (simile)   **metaphor**

The snow is a blanket of white.   **simile**   **metaphor**

Fog moves in silently like a cat with soft paws.   **simile**   **metaphor**

His smile is a ray of sunshine.   **simile**   **metaphor**

Exercise Similes and Metaphors

What comparisons can you make?

The cold air felt like _____.

His face was as red as _____.

My dreams are _____.

The stars shone like _____.

She ran as straight as _____.

The lake is a shiny _____.

Here is a poem written by a fifth-grade student. She used a web to help collect images.

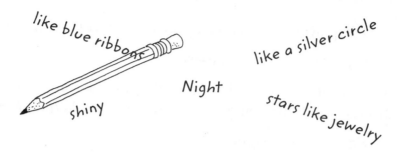

Night

The night shines like a navy blue ribbon
with jewels scattered all around.
A silver circle hangs in the sky.
I look up and I see night.

Reading Response

1. In this poem, did the author use similes and/or metaphors? What are they?

   _____

2. Which objects are compared to the night?

   _____

3. What objects do you think the jewels in the sky represent?

   _____

Here is another student poem. Notice the use of details in describing her day.

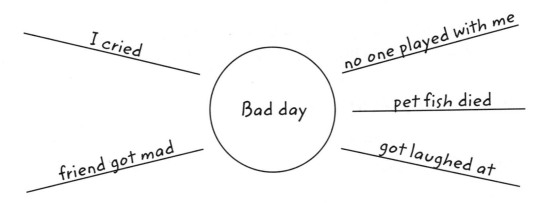

Today

I had a bad day today.

Nothing went my way today.

I cried today.

My best friend got mad at me today.

No one wanted to play today.

My fish died today.

Someone laughed at me today.

Luckily, that was all yesterday.

Reading Response

1. What word is repeated in this poem?

_____

2. Why do you think the poet chose to repeat this word?

_____

Reread the last line of the poem: "Luckily, that was all yesterday." Were you surprised? Many poems end with a surprise, or an insight that the poet discovers in the process of writing.

Exercise : Writing a Poem

Think of something to describe—perhaps a favorite season, a party, the ocean, or a busy city street. Once you have an image of your subject, think about how your senses can describe it.

- Does it have a smell?

- What does it feel like?

- What does it look like?

- What sounds does it make?

- Does it have a taste? What do you think it would taste like?

Write your descriptive phrases using similes and metaphors in the planning box below.

Remember You do not have to write in complete sentences.

Subject: _____

Sight	
Smell	
Sound	
Touch	
Taste	

Reread your descriptive phrases aloud, and underline the ones you think sound best. Write those phrases and images on the next page to make a poem, then read your poem aloud.

Title: _____

_____

_____

_____

_____

_____

_____

_____

Practice

Read through some of the poetry books you have at home, in your classroom, or at the library. Copy your favorite poem below. Have fun sharing poems!

Title: _____

_____

_____

_____

_____

_____

_____

_____

_____

Exercise   Poetry-writing Exercise

Read aloud the poem you copied, and underline your favorite line. Copy the line below. Write for five minutes using your favorite line as a starting point. Don't think too much about what you are writing, just let your imagination flow!

Favorite Line: _____

_____

_____

_____

_____

_____

_____

_____

_____

_____

_____

_____

_____

_____

_____

✓ **Editing Checklist** ✓

Read aloud your writing from the previous page. Read it again to yourself. Now, review and edit what you wrote.

❑ Make up a title for your poem. _____

❑ Underline the richest, most descriptive phrases and images.

❑ Copy the best phrases and images into the story bank below.

Story Bank 🐷

· ·

Were you surprised by what you wrote? Write about one thing that surprised you in your poem.

_____

_____

_____

Have fun sharing your poems and making illustrations to go with them, if you wish. You could also begin a poetry anthology. When you think of other writing ideas, note them in your story bank at the end of the book on page 88 to keep for later.

Chapter 3
Expository Writing

Expository writing gives information about a topic or explains something to readers. It includes details—facts, examples, reasons, and quotations—to support the topic being discussed. It could also be instructions to describe a step-by-step process. Some examples of where you will find expository writing are in textbooks, newspapers, and newsmagazines. A lot of what you read and write in school is expository.

The basic format for an expository paragraph begins with a topic sentence, followed by three or more sentences supporting that topic sentence with facts, examples, reasons, and/or quotations. The paragraph should end with a good concluding sentence to sum up, restate, or echo the paragraph topic, or to leave readers with something to think about.

Read the expository paragraph below about ants.

Those Amazing Ants!

Ants are amazing! Did you know that, like all insects, they have six legs? Each leg is made up of three joints and is very strong, allowing ants to move quickly and easily. Additionally, an ant can lift fifty times its own body weight. This would be like a one-hundred-pound person lifting 5,000 pounds! Their speed and strength allow ants to quickly move and carry what would normally seem impossible. For these reasons, ants are fascinating creatures to observe and study.

Reading Response

1. What is the topic sentence?

_____

2. Underline the supporting sentences.

3. What is the concluding sentence?

_____

_____

Writing an Expository Paragraph

Now, write your own expository paragraph, using a strong topic sentence, two or three supporting sentences, and a concluding sentence. You can write about any topic you know a lot about: your favorite book, a music group, or your town, for example.

Title: _____

_____

_____

_____

_____

_____

_____

✓ Editing Checklist ✓

❑ Underline your topic sentence.

❑ Did you write a strong conclusion? Does it make readers want to know more about your subject? Circle your concluding sentence.

Step-by-Step Processes

Expository writing can also demonstrate a *step-by-step process*, showing readers how to do something.

Read this expository paragraph describing the step-by-step process of how to make sidewalk chalk. Notice the planning steps that are used before writing the paragraph, and how the steps are arranged in a specific sequence. This form of expository writing can be applied to many other step-by-step procedures.

Planning Steps:

Materials needed:

a form to use as a mold

1 cup plaster of paris

1 cup water

powdered tempera paint

A step-by-step process:

1. Find a mold (paper cups, cardboard toilet-paper rolls, or candy molds all work well).
2. Mix 1 cup plaster of paris with 1 cup water.
3. Add paint color.
4. Pour into mold.
5. Let dry.

These words are sometimes used to help transition from one step to the next.

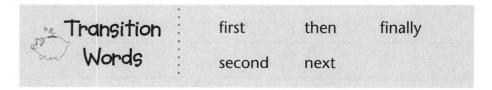

Transition Words	first	then	finally
	second	next	

How to Make Sidewalk Chalk

Sidewalk chalk is easy to make. First, gather all the materials. You will need a mold, some plaster of paris, water, and tempura paint. Second, mix one cup of plaster of paris with one cup of water. Then, add powdered color tempera paint to get the color you want. Next, let it stand for a few minutes and pour the mixture into the mold. It may take several hours or days to dry, depending on the size of the mold you use. Finally, once the mixture is dry, remove it from the mold, and let air-dry for another twenty-four hours. Now your sidewalk chalk is ready to use!

Reading Response

1. Underline the transition words used in the paragraph.

2. What is the topic sentence?

_____

3. Why do you think putting the steps in the correct sequence is so important?

_____

_____

Exercise : Step-by-Step Process

Give an example of another step-by-step process. Plan out the steps, then create an expository paragraph telling your reader how to do something. Examples are how to tie your shoes, how to get to the park, or how to use a story web.

Planning Steps:

_____

_____

_____

_____

Step-by-Step Process:

_____

_____

_____

_____

How to... _____

_____

_____

_____

_____

_____

_____

_____

Now switch papers with a partner and see if you can follow the other person's step-by-step directions.

Summaries

You have probably been asked to write *summaries* for school assignments or tests. A *summary* includes the main idea and the most important supporting details of a written piece. It should be written in your own words and be very brief, focusing on only the main idea. It may take several sentences or in some cases just one. The process of writing a summary can help you better understand the material you read.

Here are some steps to guide you:

1. Carefully read the written piece.

2. Identify the main idea.

3. Identify supporting details.

4. Write your summary. Be sure to use your own words.

Guidelines:
1. The first sentence should include the main idea.
2. Add most important details in a logical sequence.
3. Rewrite the summary to make it as brief as possible, but also complete.

Read this paragraph and the summary below about how the teddy bear got its name.

How "Teddy's Bear" Got Its Name

On November 14, 1902, Theodore "Teddy" Roosevelt, the twenty-sixth president of the United States, went on a hunting trip as a relaxing break from his presidential duties. Thinking it would please the president, the other hunters tied a bear to a tree as an easy target, so Roosevelt could go home with a trophy. Instead, he surprised everyone by ordering that the bear be set free.

A newspaper reporter heard the story, and soon a childlike cartoon appeared in papers nationwide, showing the president freeing a helpless cub. Roosevelt's popularity soared as a result. A toymaker named Mitchom designed a little bear and called it "Teddy's Bear." It became very popular, and still is. Today, collecting teddy bears is a hobby shared by many children and adults.

Summary:

The teddy bear was designed and named for Teddy Roosevelt, the twenty-sixth president of the United States. He freed a real bear during a hunting trip in 1902, and this made him very well-liked. A toymaker created a stuffed bear and called it "Teddy's Bear," which is the teddy bear that is still popular today.

Reading Response

1. In your own words, what is the main idea of the paragraph?

_____

_____

2. List three important details from the summary.

_____

_____

Writing Summaries

Select a paragraph or two from your science or social studies textbook. Read it carefully several times. Write a summary of the passage using the guidelines listed on page 44. Make sure you include the main idea and the most important supporting details. Be as brief, but accurate, as possible.

Summary:

_____

_____

_____

_____

_____

_____

_____

✓ Editing Checklist ✓

❏ Is the main idea of the paragraph clear in your summary?

❏ List three important details from the summary.

_____

_____

Information Reports

In school, you will write information reports. To plan your information report you will need to gather facts and data from various sources such as books, magazines, the Internet, and personal interviews. Writing the report involves presenting and summarizing information in your own words. Information reports are structured with a beginning main idea, middle supporting information, then an ending conclusion to sum up your information or leave your reader with something to think about.

Narrowing Your Topic

 **Remember** When choosing a topic for your report, try to narrow the subject. For example, the paragraph on page 45 is specifically written about how the teddy bear got its name, not about bears in general.

The planning charts below show examples of how to narrow a topic before writing.

Steps to help narrow down a topic:

Example 1:

Step 1:	animals
Step 2:	raccoon
Step 3:	raccoons' habits
Step 4:	how raccoons find food

Example 2:

Step 1:	plants
Step 2:	flowers
Step 3:	dandelions
Step 4:	how dandelions spread their seeds

Narrowing a Topic

Now it's your turn to narrow a topic. Start with a broad topic for Step 1, and narrow it down in Steps 2, 3, and 4.

Step 1:	
Step 2:	
Step 3:	
Step 4:	

Final Topic: _____

Step 1:	
Step 2:	
Step 3:	
Step 4:	

Final Topic: _____

Step 1:	
Step 2:	
Step 3:	
Step 4:	

Final Topic: _____

Compare and Contrast

One way to organize an information report is to describe how two things are alike and how they are different. This can lead to a greater understanding of both.

When comparing similarities and differences it helps to use a chart like the *Venn diagram* modeled below. A Venn diagram shows similarities in the overlapping circles in the middle, and differences in the outer circles.

Topic: Compare and Contrast Augusta, Maine, and Tallahassee, Florida

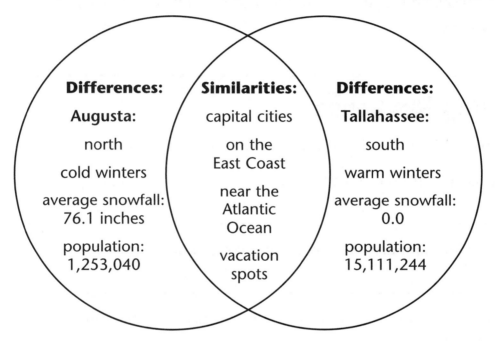

Differences:

Augusta:

north

cold winters

average snowfall: 76.1 inches

population: 1,253,040

Similarities:

capital cities

on the East Coast

near the Atlantic Ocean

vacation spots

Differences:

Tallahassee:

south

warm winters

average snowfall: 0.0

population: 15,111,244

Transition words to help write the paragraph:

Transition Words	however	on the other hand	compared to
	but	whereas	

Tallahassee versus Augusta

Both capital cities Tallahassee, Florida, and Augusta, Maine, are located on the East Coast of the United States. Augusta is in the north and Tallahassee is in the south. However, they both are not far from the Atlantic Ocean and are popular vacation spots. Tallahassee usually has warm, balmy weather and no snow, whereas Augusta has very cold winters and averages 76.1 inches of snow each year. Another difference is Tallahassee's population of about 15,111,000 compared to Augusta, which has a population only of about 1,253,000. Both of these state capitals offer appealing alternatives as a place to live or visit.

Reading Response

1. Underline the transition words used in the paragraph.

2. What is one difference between Tallahassee and Augusta?

   _____

3. What is one similarity between Tallahassee and Augusta?

   _____

4. Think of one difference between your own state capital and Tallahassee or Augusta.

   _____

5. Think of one similarity between your own state capital and Tallahassee or Augusta.

   _____

Exercise Compare and Contrast

Choose two places or foods to compare and contrast. Use the chart on the next page to list similarities and differences to help you plan. Remember to use the transition words to help write your paragraph.

Differences: **Similarities:** **Differences:**

Comparing: _____ **with:** _____

_____

_____

_____

_____

_____

_____

_____

_____

_____

✓ **Editing Checklist** ✓

❏ Did you show similarities between your subjects?

❏ Did you show their differences?

❏ Did you write a concluding sentence?

Compare and Contrast through Journal Writing

A journal can be another form of expository writing. It is one way to keep a daily record of thoughts, feelings, ideas, and events. This lends itself well to showing similarities and differences. For example, a journal could show how different your life would have been at another time in history, but would also point out some basic similarities. This could be a fun approach to studying the past. The journal entries below compare and contrast a day in the life of a frontier child and a modern-day child.

September 22, 1860

At dawn, my brother and I rolled up our bedclothes and climbed out of our covered wagon to gather wood for a fire. I milked the cow for fresh milk to put on our porridge. Then, while Mom cooked over the campfire, I fed the horses. It was a chilly fall day, so we stayed wrapped in blankets while eating breakfast. Afterwards, Dad and my brother hitched the horses to the wagon so we could continue our trip West. I stayed with Mom to help pack. We were still many days away from our destination. Even though we were tired at the end of the day, we couldn't wait to sit down to play with our dog, then climb under the covers to read.

September 22, 2003

My brother and I had to get up early this morning to do our chores. Each day, I take out the trash, and my brother feeds the dog. Dad heated up some yummy muffins in the microwave, and put strawberries on our cereal for breakfast. We met our friends at the bus just in time to hop on. It was a chilly fall morning, but luckily the bus was heated. We got to school just in time for homeroom. After a busy day at school, I went to soccer practice and my brother went to karate. I called Mom on my cell phone to say hi, since I knew she'd be working late. Even though we were tired when we got home, we couldn't wait to play with our dog and computer games.

Reading Response

1. In the chart below, list what is *similar* and what is *different* about the journal writers' lives.

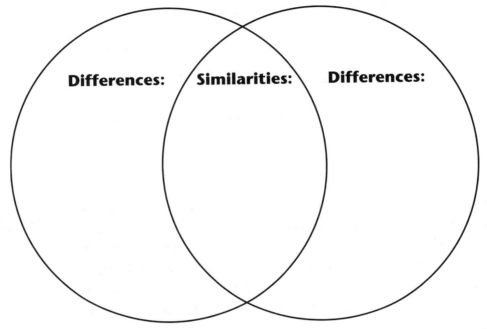

Differences: **Similarities:**   **Differences:**

2. List three words that are clearly from the present day.

_____

✎ Practice

Now write brief summaries of the two journals.

September 22, 1860:

_____

_____

_____

_____

_____

_____

September 22, 2003:

_____

_____

_____

_____

_____

_____

⌐ Exercise ⌐ Journal Writing

Now it's your turn to write two journal entries to show the similarities and differences in your life compared to a child from a time in history. One journal will be about a day in your life in the present, and one will be about a day in your life as if you were living in the past. Make sure to gather enough facts so the similarities and differences are clear. You could consider clothing, school, communication, transportation, home life, traditions, recreation, etc.

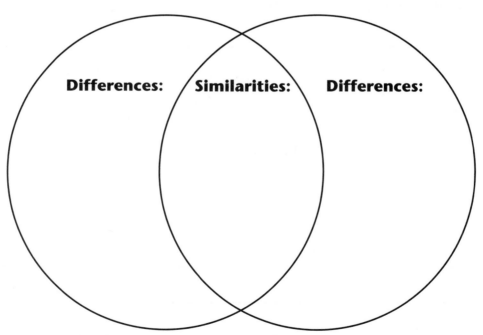

Differences: **Similarities:**   **Differences:**

Journal Entries

Past:

_____

_____

_____

_____

_____

_____

_____

Present:

_____

_____

_____

_____

_____

_____

_____

✔ Editing Checklist ✔

❑ Did you use the Venn diagram to plan?

❑ Did you use enough examples to make the similarities and differences clear?

❑ Did writing these paragraphs help you learn historical facts?

Planning a Multiparagraph Information Report

Your information report will often need to be longer than one paragraph in order to show all the facts and details you've gathered about your topic. In these cases, you will need to write a *multiparagraph information report*. In order to plan a multiparagraph information report you should:

1. Choose a topic and narrow it.

2. Think of some questions you would like answered about the topic.

3. Write each question across the top of a 3x5 notecard, or enter it into a computer.

4. Gather information from resources (books, magazines, newspapers, the Internet, people, etc.) to find answers to your questions. Write the information on notecards or add it to your computer file. Include facts, examples, and quotes.

5. Organize notecards or computer files so the information is in logical order. Each question can serve as a topic for a paragraph.

 **Remember** Be sure to keep track of where you found your information, including names and page numbers or Web addresses.

Writing a Multiparagraph Information Report

Good News! A multiparagraph report uses the same basic format for each paragraph.

1. Topic Sentence: clearly introduces the topic

2. Body: three or four supporting sentences about the topic

3. Concluding Sentence: sums up the information or leads into the next paragraph

In a multiparagraph report, each paragraph has its own job.

Beginning: Introduction

Middle: Support

End: Conclusion

Beginning: Introduction – Start with something interesting to grab the reader's attention (a quotation, an interesting fact, a question) and introduce the topic.

Middle: Support – Include facts, examples, and possibly quotes to support the subject. This information should be in a logical order.

End: Conclusion – Summarize the ideas that have been covered in the report. It could explain why this subject is memorable or important.

Your information report also needs to have a *title* to catch your readers' attention and tell what they are about to learn. The title should be short—only a few words—and should be informative but interesting. When you're choosing a title, think of something you would want to read.

 **Remember** Don't forget to capitalize every word in the title, except for articles in the middle of the title (a, an, the) and prepositions (with, of, by, for, etc.).

Look at the planning notecards, and then read the multiparagraph information report on the next page.

When do we see fireflies?
night
warm weather

Why do fireflies light up?
signal
attracts mate

How do fireflies light up?
chemical reaction in dark
oxygen

Title:
Fireflies Are Amazing
Glowing Fireflies
Firefly Magic

Firefly Magic

Have you ever seen fireflies flicker and dart around in the night? If you're outside on a balmy night and see fireflies flashing, it looks magical. They seem to signal and talk to one another. All we see is their little light zooming around in the darkness.

The light is actually the firefly's signal. It is used to attract a mate. The male firefly darts around looking for the female's signal. The light is caused by a chemical reaction in the firefly that is visible in the dark. As the firefly breathes in oxygen, the light becomes stronger.

This summer, watch for the glow of the firefly. The ability of such a small insect to light up is a rare and fascinating feat of nature. Fireflies are fun to watch, and you might be tempted to catch some. However, you should let them go again, for they are truly wondrous insects.

Reading Response

1. What did the author ask in the first sentence to catch your attention?

   _____

2. Write one fact that clearly explains the firefly's light.

   _____

3. What comment in the concluding paragraph best emphasizes the importance of the firefly?

   _____

   _____

✎ Practice

Write a summary for this report. (review summary definition on page 44)

_____

_____

_____

⋮ Exercise ⋮ Writing a Multiparagraph Report

This exercise will include planning and writing a multiparagraph report on the history of your town's name. Use resources like the library, your textbooks, and the Internet to research the subject. Review pages 56 and 57, which show the format for a multi-paragraph report. Use the Know, Want, Learn chart on page 82 to plan your report. Then, you are ready to begin your report. Attach extra sheets of paper to this page for more room to write.

Beginning: Introduction

Middle: Support paragraph/paragraphs

End: Conclusion

Title: _____

_____

_____

_____

_____

_____

_____

✔ Editing Checklist ✔

❑ Did you include explanations to support your facts?

❑ Did you use a variety of sources to research your topic?

Commas

When you add detail to your writing, commas are very useful. Commas help make your writing clearer, and tell readers to make a brief pause in their reading. They also help by grouping words to make your writing easier to read.

In your writing, commas are used for:

- lists
- combining sentences

Lists

Commas are used to separate items in a list. These items might be objects or actions. Also, add a comma before the word "and" when listing items in a sentence. This is called a *serial comma*.

Example:

In the summer, Charlie loves swimming in his neighbor's pool, visiting his grandma, hiking with his uncle John, and playing card games with his cousins.

Combining Sentences

Two complete sentences (two independent clauses) can be combined with a joining word to make one interesting sentence. These joining words are *conjunctions*. Always use a comma between two independent clauses that are joined by conjunctions.

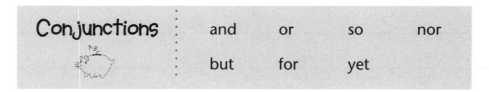

Conjunctions	and	or	so	nor
	but	for	yet	

Example:

Two short choppy sentences:

Salt marshes are endangered. We have to try to preserve them.

Combined sentence:

Salt marshes are endangered, so we have to try to preserve them.

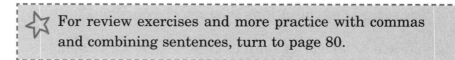

☆ For review exercises and more practice with commas and combining sentences, turn to page 80.

Chapter 4
Persuasive Writing

The purpose of persuasive writing is to convince someone to think in a certain way, do something, or buy something. You might find persuasive writing in newspaper editorials, magazine articles, letters, and advertisements. Before you write in the persuasive writing style, you need to think about your audience and your specific purpose for writing.

Audience

Will you be trying to persuade your classmates, a teacher, a parent, or a politician? How can you grab their interest? Different audiences could change how you write. For example, you might use different words if you were writing to your younger brother than if you were writing to your teacher.

Purpose

Keeping your audience in mind, what is your specific purpose? For example, do you want to encourage the town to build a new community center? Do you want to convince teachers to give you a longer lunch break?

Facts and Opinions

When we write persuasively, we often use facts and opinions. A *fact* is a piece of information that can be proven. An *opinion* is an idea that a person believes.

	Fact	Opinion
Strawberries	Strawberries are red fruits.	Strawberries are delicious.
Bicycles	Bicycles have two wheels.	Bicycles are fun to ride.

It is important to support an opinion with reasons. Reasons can include facts, justifications, explanations, and supported observations.

 Telling your reader why you believe something is more persuasive than just stating your opinion.

The words below are useful for writing opinions:

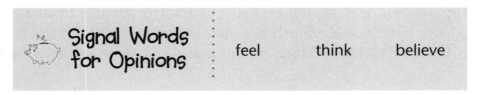

Signal Words for Opinions   feel   think   believe

Exercise Facts and Opinions

Fill in a fact and opinion for the last three items:

Subject	Fact	Opinion
baseball and soccer	Baseball and soccer are sports.	Baseball is more exciting than soccer.
art	Art includes painting and sculpting.	All schools should offer art.
elephants 	Elephants _____ _____	_____ _____
cars	Cars _____ _____	_____ _____
the moon	The moon _____ _____	_____ _____

Basic ingredients of a persuasive piece:

1. A strong beginning grabs the reader's attention and introduces the writer's purpose or position. This might be an opinion, a fact, a question, or a quotation.

2. Reasons and facts support your position.

3. Mention the differing opinion, and explain why you don't agree.

4. A strong closing leaves the reader with a clear memory of how you feel and why. Your ending might offer a plan of action, or encourage others to join in the cause.

Read the two paragraphs below. Notice how each paragraph is about the same topic, but is directed at a different audience. The first sentence in each paragraph is written to catch the reader's attention.

Facts:	Opinions:	Differing opinion:
save trees	easy to do	too expensive
create jobs	makes a difference	too time-consuming
reuses useful material	responsibility	

Why Recycling Is Right: Passage 1

Recycling could save many beautiful trees. By simply recycling paper, our town could make a huge impact and contribute to helping the environment. Initially it would be expensive to set up a recycling center, but the benefits would make it worthwhile. Recycling creates new jobs as well as reuses useful material. If each household took all its used newspapers and white paper supplies to the recycling center just once a week, it could make a difference. We would all feel good to know that, as a community, we are taking part in saving trees. I believe it is our civic responsibility.

Why Recycling Is Right: Passage 2

Did you know that our school uses two hundred reams of paper each week? Because we use so much paper at school, it is a perfect place to set up a paper recycling program. Statistics show that recycling paper has saved millions of trees. Even though people think it would take too much time, it would be easy for each classroom to have a recycling basket for used white paper goods. We could rotate the responsibility of collecting and emptying the baskets. The recycling center has even agreed to pick up our paper each week. I think it is extremely important for our school to set a good example for others. Please help save our trees!

Reading Response

1. Do you think the first paragraph was written for adults or kids?

_____

2. Do you think the second paragraph was written for adults or kids?

_____

3. Write one opinion and two supporting facts from both paragraphs.

Paragraph 1: Opinion _____

Paragraph 1: Supporting Facts _____

_____

Paragraph 2: Opinion _____

Paragraph 2: Supporting Facts _____

_____

4. What opposing opinion does the writer present?

Paragraph 1: _____

_____

Paragraph 2: _____

_____

5. What was the plan of action suggested in the paragraphs?

Paragraph 1: _____

_____

Paragraph 2: _____

_____

Exercise Persuasive Writing

Pick one of the topics listed below or think up your own. Decide how you feel about it, and try to persuade your reader to agree with you. Remember to narrow your topic.

Wearing uniforms at school

Dogs on leashes

Healthful eating

Exercise

Sports stars as role models

Favorite type of music

School rules

Homework

Recess

Once you have chosen a topic, use the chart below to plan your writing.

Topic or Issue: _____

Audience: _____

Purpose: _____

Opinions	Reasons or facts to support opinion	Action your readers could take

Remember Try to combine short sentences using conjunctions and commas.

Write your paragraph, then share it with a partner.

Title: _____

_____

_____

_____

_____

_____

_____

_____

_____

_____

✓ Editing Checklist ✓

❑ Is the purpose clear to your audience?

❑ Did you include facts and reasons to support your opinion?

❑ Did you offer a suggestion of some action?

Now, using the same planning chart above, rewrite your paragraph addressing a different audience (friend, parent, politician, classmate, teacher, etc.)

Title: _____

_____

_____

_____

_____

_____

_____

How are your paragraphs different?

_____

_____

_____

_____

_____

_____

Persuasive Letter

Another type of persuasive writing is a *persuasive letter*. These include letters to the editor of a magazine or newspaper, and letters to a business, politician, family member, or friend. Below is a multiparagraph persuasive letter.

Read this persuasive letter. Pay attention to the writer's purpose, use of language for the audience, supporting facts and opinions, and call to action.

South Street Elementary School
100 South Street,
City, State, Zip Code, USA

March 2, 2004

State Representative Henriquez
State House
Capital City, State, Zip Code, USA

Dear Representative:

When you were younger, did you ever feel strongly about something that seemed unfair, and wish you could make a difference? Well, my class and I have an issue we feel frustrated with, and we are writing to ask for your help. We have been studying how the early European settlers treated Native Americans unfairly. The settlers took away their land and brought diseases that killed many Native Americans. It seems to us that, even today, their human rights are not always treated with enough respect.

We have written a proposal to organize students across the country to join in the effort to improve the conditions on Native American reservations. We would like the government to provide more money for schools, books, and housing on the reservations. There are over one hundred reservations in the United States, and many of them have poor living conditions and not enough money for education. Some people think that the government should not have to help the Native Americans, but we think they should receive aid because of the abuses they suffered. We feel this is an area in which students' voices could make a difference.

What we are asking you to do is to give your support by reviewing our proposal and suggesting what our next step should be. We feel that, with your help, our dream of a good education and better living conditions on the reservations could come true. We hope you feel as strongly as we do about this issue, and will want to be involved. We can't do it alone!

Sincerely,

Ms. Shield's class

Reading Response

1. What is the purpose of this letter?

_____

_____

2. What do you think are the most convincing points of the letter?

_____

_____

3. What words used by the writer show that the letter is to a government official, rather than a classmate?

_____

_____

Exercise Persuasive Letter

Now it's your turn to write a persuasive letter. Convince your parents, a teacher, the head of a company, or a politician about something you feel strongly, in a multiparagraph letter. Examples include education, gun control, and the environment. First, decide to whom you are going to write, then, what you are trying to convince them to do, think, or believe.

Remember When choosing an idea or issue, consider:

- Purpose
- Audience
- What specific action do you want the reader to take?
- Gather facts and reasons to support your position.

Use this format:

Beginning: Introduction

Begin with an opening to grab the reader's attention and establish a bond. Introduce the issue and state your opinion, briefly showing the facts and reasons to support your opinion.

Middle: Support Paragraph or Paragraphs

Explain your supporting facts and reasons, and give further detail.

End: Conclusion

Present a summary, and leave your readers with a call to action.

Use the box below to collect facts and reasons to support your opinion.

Topic:

_____

Attention-catching first sentence:

_____

Facts	Opinions and reasons to support facts	Call to action

☆ For a reminder of correct letter-writing format, turn to page 83.

Dear _____:

_____

_____

_____

_____

_____

_____

_____

_____

_____

_____

_____

_____

Sincerely,

_____

✓ Editing Checklist ✓

❑ Did you use a multiparagraph format?

❑ Do you think your letter would convince someone who disagreed with you? If so, why?

_____

_____

Advertisements

Advertisements are a kind of persuasive writing we hear and see all the time. The purpose of ads is to persuade people that they need a product or a service. Advertisers have to choose their words very carefully based on who they want to buy their product—their audience. Think of some places you might hear and see ads.

Many ads:

1. Begin with a dynamic opening to grab the audience's attention and identify the product.

2. Describe the product's benefits, giving opinions and supportive facts as evidence that the advertiser's opinion is trustworthy.

3. End with a request for the audience to buy the product.

Can you think of any ads that follow this format?

Cause and Effect in Advertising

When one thing happens that makes something else happen, it is called *cause and effect*. Many advertisers use cause and effect to show what will happen if the audience does—or does not—buy their product.

Examples:

Advertisement: If you fall down and land on your knee, your knee might swell if you aren't wearing Super Safe Skating Pads!

Cause: falling on your knee without wearing kneepads

Effect: swelling of your knee

Advertisement: Buy Crazy Cat Jeans to be the coolest kid in your class!

Cause: buying Crazy Cat Jeans

Effect: becoming the most fashionable kid in your class

Read the text of this television advertisement. Think about what the advertiser is selling, to whom it is being sold, and why.

Cool Country toothpaste is the best! You need this special fluoride treatment to protect your teeth from decay. Guarding against cavities is especially important for your children. Our teeth tend to yellow with age, but also if we drink coffee or other substances that stain. If you use Cool Country and brush at least twice a day, your teeth will be whiter and healthier, and your mouth will feel fresher than ever before. Everyone loves a dazzling smile, so rush out and buy some Cool Country today!

Now talk with a partner about the facts and opinions in the toothpaste ad.

Reading Response

1. What does the advertiser say *causes* teeth to yellow?

   _____

2. What are two of the *effects* of using Cool Country, according to the advertiser?

   _____

3. Write one fact and one opinion from the toothpaste ad.

   Fact

   _____

   Opinion

   _____

4. Whom do you think this ad was written for?

   _____

Sometimes opinions are written to sound like fact. Recognizing the difference between facts and opinions helps you make a better judgment about the content of the ad.

Read the ad below.

Do you ever dream of being a great athlete? Well, eating Score Cereal can make that dream come true. Score Cereal has a daily supply of vitamins B, D, and E in every bowl! Not only will you be stronger, but the vitamin enrichment will give you increased stamina so you can practice longer. In just a few days you will notice a difference. Remember: Eat Score and score!

Eat *SCORE* and score!

Reading Response

1. Who does the advertiser target as the audience for this ad?

   _____

2. What is the purpose of the first sentence?

   _____

3. What do you think is actually an opinion that is made to sound like a fact?

   _____

4. What do you think is probably a fact? How could you find out?

   _____

   _____

The words you choose are important in persuasive writing. An ad for a toy, for example, would use different words than an ad for a kitchen cleanser. One wishes to attract a child, the other, an adult. Look at the lists below:

Toy:	Kitchen cleanser:
fast	clean
fun	inexpensive
colorful	scented
exciting	fresh

Think of a product that both a child and an adult might want to buy. Examples include a family car, lunchtime snack, or new shirt. Think of different words you would use to describe the product in an advertisement, to appeal to different audiences.

Product _____

Words for adults	**Words for kids**
_____	_____
_____	_____
_____	_____
_____	_____

⌇ Exercise ⌇ Writing an Ad

Think of an item or product that you love, like a favorite book, game, or type of pet. Now, write an ad to convince others to want it, too. Use the chart on the next page to plan.

Item or Product	Audience	Purpose	Facts

Opinions	Convincing Reasons	Effective Word Choices

Before you start to write, draw a picture for your ad. Write a *caption* underneath it that sums up the best points/strongest reasons to buy the product. A caption is a short sentence or phrase to describe your product. It can also be a *slogan* or *catchphrase* the audience automatically associates with a specific product.

Caption: _____

Now you are ready to write your ad!

Remember

1. Begin with a dynamic opening to grab the reader's attention. Identify your product.

2. Describe the product's benefits, using opinions and supportive facts as evidence that your opinion is trustworthy.

3. End with a call to action, to buy the product.

_____

_____

_____

_____

_____

_____

_____

_____

_____

✔ Editing Checklist ✔

❑ Will your audience know what your product is and does?

❑ Did you use interesting words to make your ad informational and lively?

❑ What makes your ad convincing enough to make others want to buy your product?

_____

_____

Dialogue

New Speakers, New Paragraphs

When there is a new paragraph, the reader generally knows that a different person is speaking.

In the sentences below, put a check where paragraph changes should be. Then, rewrite the dialogue. Be sure to start a new paragraph each time the speaker changes.

Remember Don't forget to indent every new paragraph.

"Allie, did you finish your homework?" "Not yet, Marta. I need help on my map, so it is taking extra time. Are you done?" "Yes, I just finished. Can I help you?"

_____

_____

_____

_____

_____

Check the above dialogue. Make sure that every time there is a new speaker, you begin a new line and paragraph.

Dialogue can show personality traits about the people speaking.

✎ Practice

Read the following example and try to picture the two speakers.

"But I don't want to!" he screamed.

"Listen, James, you must return the book today," Ms. Jones said firmly.

"Please let me keep it for another day," he pleaded.

"James, someone else may want the book," said Ms. Jones patiently. "Please return it to the library by the end of the day."

Reading Response

1. How would you describe James?

   _____

2. How would you describe Ms. Jones?

   _____

Remember When punctuating dialogue:

- Put quotation marks before the first word spoken and after the last word spoken.
- Use commas to separate spoken words from the speaker.
- Capitalize the first word after the quotation mark at the beginning of a sentence.
- If the quotation is interrupted midsentence, the first letter of the second clause is lowercase.
- Punctuation marks go <u>inside</u> the quotation marks.

✎ Practice

Read the following and circle the five points to remember when punctuating dialogue.

"The cat," said Jill, "ran up that tree."

Commas

Remember Commas indicate a short pause.

Commas are used for

- Lists

- Combining sentences

Lists

Commas are used to separate items in a list. These items might be objects or actions. Add a comma before the word "and" when listing items in a sentence. This is called a *serial comma*.

Exercise : Placing Commas

In the following sentences, insert commas where needed.

1. Dad went to buy dinner. He needed bread lettuce tomatoes hamburger and fruit for dessert.

2. Jenny would like to go skiing in the winter hiking and water skiing in the summer and fishing in the spring.

3. Aunt Maggie Uncle Pete Uncle Ralph Helena Grandma and Grandpop are all coming to spend the weekend with us.

4. After school Juanita goes to band practice picks up her brother from the babysitter does her homework and eats dinner with her family.

Exercise : Using Commas in Sentences

Write three of your own sentences below, showing that you know where to use a comma when listing things.

1. Write a complete sentence listing four of your favorite foods.

_____

_____

2. Write a complete sentence including three places you'd like to visit.

_____

_____

3. Write a complete sentence listing five things you might pack for a weekend trip.

_____

_____

_____

Combining Sentences

Two complete sentences (two independent clauses) can be combined with a joining word to make one interesting sentence. These joining words are *conjunctions*. Always use a comma between two independent clauses that are joined by conjunctions.

Conjunctions	and	or	so	nor
	but	for	yet	

Examples:

Two short choppy sentences:

Maddy was tired. Her sister wanted to play cards.

Combined sentences:

Maddy was tired, but her sister wanted to play cards.

Two short choppy sentences:

Ricky was proud. He won the spelling bee.

Ricky was proud, because he won the spelling bee.

✎ Practice

Underline the conjunctions in the two examples above.

In the following sentences, underline the conjunctions, then insert commas where needed. If you are unsure, review the examples on page 81.

1. Jeff loves baseball but his older brother prefers soccer.

2. We'll get there by car yet you'll go by bus.

3. Do you want to read or shall we play a board game?

4. The library was too warm so we read our books outside on the bench.

5. The rain missed getting them wet as the people were slouched over.

Write four examples of combining two sentences.

1. _____

2. _____

3. _____

4. _____

Know, Want, Learn chart

A Know, Want, Learn chart (also called a KWL chart) is one example of a graphic organizer you can use to help sort out your thoughts. A KWL chart shows what you **KNOW** and **WANT to know** about a topic, and also asks what you **LEARNED** by researching the subject.

Subject: _____

K What I **KNOW**	**W** What I **WANT** to know	**L** What I **LEARNED**

Sample Letter

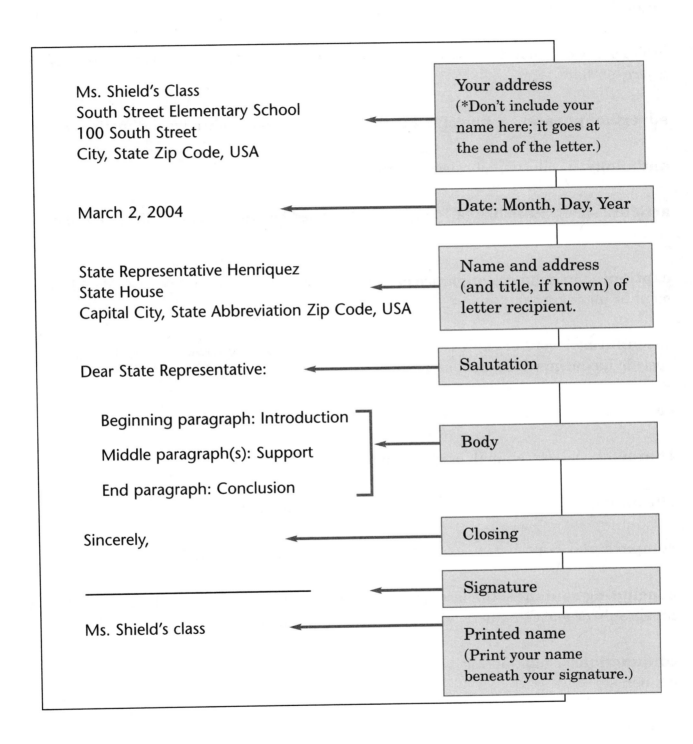

Ms. Shield's Class
South Street Elementary School
100 South Street
City, State Zip Code, USA

<- Your address (*Don't include your name here; it goes at the end of the letter.)

March 2, 2004

<- Date: Month, Day, Year

State Representative Henriquez
State House
Capital City, State Abbreviation Zip Code, USA

<- Name and address (and title, if known) of letter recipient.

Dear State Representative:

<- Salutation

Beginning paragraph: Introduction

Middle paragraph(s): Support

End paragraph: Conclusion

<- Body

Sincerely,

<- Closing

_____

<- Signature

Ms. Shield's class

<- Printed name (Print your name beneath your signature.)

Glossary

adjective: a word that describes a noun

adverb: a word that describes a verb, adjective, or another adverb; usually tells *when, where,* or *how*

adverbial phrase: a group of words that describe a verb, adjective, or another adverb

anthology: a collection of selected writings

articles: small words like "a," "an," and "the" used before nouns that help describe them

caption: short sentence or phrase describing or explaining an image (usually advertisement or photograph)

catchphrase: word or expression used repeatedly to automatically associate the specific language with a person, product, or idea

cause and effect: something happening and the result of that event

character: person, animal, or object in a story

chronological order: events shown in the order they happened

compare and contrast: to examine how things are similar and different

concluding sentence: the last sentence of a paragraph; sums up or leads into the next paragraph, or leaves readers with something to think about

conjunctions: small linking words that join two parts of a sentence (and, but, or, yet, for, nor, so)

conveyed: shown through writing, speaking, or movement

descriptive writing: focuses on the five senses

dialogue: a conversation between two or more people in a story

evoke: make someone feel a certain way through sensory reminders

explanations: reasons that show why something happened

expository writing: shows something new or explains something to the readers

fact: a piece of information that can be proven

fictional narrative: story made up by the author

first-person: story is told from the author/narrator's point of view (I, my, me, us, we, our)

five Ws: who, what, where, when, why

independent clause: a group of words including both a subject and a verb

information report: written piece that involves researching and summarizing facts

justification: the proof or reason behind an action, behavior, or event

"Know, Want, Learn" (KWL) chart: diagram to help organize ideas by showing what the author knows, wants to know, and has learned through research

lead: the opening of a news story (often the first line) that tells the main idea

metaphor: direct, unexpected comparison between two things

multiparagraph information report: an information report involving more than one paragraph

narrative: story (real or imaginary) with a beginning, middle, and end

narrative writing: tells the story of something or someone real or imaginary

narrator: the person whose voice is telling the story to readers

nonfiction narrative: type of story involving things that really happened

observation: a judgment based on something seen or experienced

opinion: how a person feels about something

opposing: opposite, disagreeing

paragraph sign (¶): editing symbol that indicates where a new paragraph should begin

personal narrative: writing that tells a true story about the author

persuasive writing: writing used to convince readers of the author's point of view

plot: the action of the story, often based on a central problem to solve

plot line: shows the main events of the story, from beginning to climax to resolution

poetry: usually short writings (sometimes rhyming) that reflect the essence of a feeling, experience, or idea

position: the way someone feels about something

preposition: small linking word that shows the relationship between other words in the sentence (with, of, by, for, between, etc.)

purpose: reason for action

quotation: something said or written by someone else and reused by an author, giving credit to the original writer/speaker

relayed: the passing along of a message

senses: sight, sound, smell, touch, taste

sensory: relating to the senses

sequence: the order of events

serial comma: the comma used just before the word "and" in a list (dogs, cats, and chickens)

setting: the backdrop of a story; where and when the story takes place

simile: an indirect, unexpected comparison between two things using the words "like" or "as" to connect them

slogan: brief, attention-catching phrase, sometimes used in advertisements

specific: particular; narrowed-down

step-by-step process: chronological directions to complete a task

summary: short writing that tells the main points of a longer piece, in the author's own words

supporting sentences: sentences that strengthen the main idea of the writing

third-person: narration of a story told by someone other than the main character ("he," "him," "she," "her," "they," "them," and "their")

title: few words at the top of the page that tell readers what the story is about

topic sentence: the main sentence that tells what the writing is about

transition: to move from one thing or idea to another related thing or idea

trustworthy: dependable, true

Venn diagram: type of graphic organizer using overlapping circles to reflect similarities and differences

verbs: "action words" or "being words"

Story Bank

Story Bank